COMING INTO MY OWN AS A SOCIAL WORKER

Introduction

I want to thank you and congratulate you for downloading or ordering the book, *"Coming Into My Own: As a Social Worker"*.

This book is dedicated in memory of my sister Shirley Ann Carlisle. It contains my sister's journey to achieve her goal to become a social worker. This book tells the story of her life growing up in the 60's and how it affects her decisions in life. It provides details on what takes place during the 60's such as, Martin L. King death, riots, and how the community changes as well as her contributions to help change school curriculum for Black American History.

Shirley Carlisle-Bryson belonged to Alpha Zeta Delta, a Chapter of Phi Theta Kappa. This organization was for students who could maintain a 3.2 GPA. Shirley Carlisle-Bryson was born May 10, 1952 in Bessemer, Alabama. She will be remembered as being an extremely calm, tranquil woman who was not easily flustered. At the time of her illness, she was attending Cleveland

State University where she was studying (and completed) to become a social worker. Shirley was a highly intelligent individual with a 4.0 grade point average, extremely computer literate, and highly trained. Shirley was also a volunteer tutor for the Cleveland School System.

Shirley departed life on January 25, 2005, at that time she left; three brother, Jack, Ronald (deceased) and Troy, two sisters, Patricia and Brenda; six nieces Davera, Kristin, Shannon, Toni, Alahjanai and Kaylah; four nephews, Dionta, Akil, Akeem and Christian. To add, her mom who departed before her, Caldonia (deceased) and father Jack Carlisle (deceased) She was imposed inspiration to all whose life she touched. Shirley is greatly and immeasurably missed.

Thanks again for ordering this book. I hope you enjoy it!

Chapter 1
Pursuing a dream

Social Work was a dream of mine for some time that I'm just now beginning to realize. The seeds were actually planted when I graduated from high school quit a few years ago. I didn't know very much about the field of social work at the time nor did I realize the various disciplines within the field of social work. As a child growing up in the 60's, it wouldn't be very long before I would become keenly aware of the many disparities that existed between the majority (white) population and minorities. And, as an African American female, it was impossible to live in this country and not realize there were quite a few social issues that affected me that I would have to deal with.

Oh, don't get me wrong, I had a wonderful childhood growing up in the inner city in the 60's. Our neighborhoods were more cohesive and stronger; and neighbors actually helped neighbors in those days. We actually knew what mutual aid was and practiced it on a daily basis especially when a neighbor was sick or shut in. Neighbors actually watched out for each other's children and we knew all our neighbors on the street, not just those directly in front of us. In those days, we didn't have to venture further than the corner of our street in order to find an ice cream parlor, dry cleaners, hardware store, beauty parlor or bakery.

In fact, there was a bakery at the corner of our street named "Mary's Bakery" that just happened to be owned by a very nice White lady. I thought we were living a pretty good life until I learned through our newspapers what was really happening to Black people in the southern states of Alabama and Mississippi.

I was only a teenager but could hardly believe Whites had so much hatred for blacks. After all, our parents never taught us to hate them so why on earth did they hate us so. What in the world did we do to deserve such hatred, I asked myself. These were the days when Martin Luther King, Jr. was leading the fight for our civil rights and many people were up in arms about the mistreatment of Black people especially the Black Nationalists. The Black Nationalists was a militant group determined to take on the White power structure, and our community would become the backdrop for a vicious and bloody battle between them and the police.

Chapter 2
Paying homage to Martin Luther King, Jr.

Martin's assassination would touch off riots in every major metropolitan city and life would never be the same. I wasn't able to take up the fight but these events had a profound effect on the way I would view our country for quite awhile. And when Martin Luther King, Jr. was killed, his courage would ignite a whole high school whose students were fed up with the status quo.

At first, all we wanted was to go to Public Square and hear the tribute to honor Martin Luther King, Jr. Of course, the administration turned us down but we would not be denied this right to pay homage to such a great humanitarian. We were told "they" could not give us permission, but if we went peacefully, no one would be punished for leaving. Needless to say, we went and it was beautiful and peaceful eulogy but we realized things would have to change. And they did.

The year before I graduated high school, the Black student body demanded

African American history courses and a change in the curriculum. Sadly, there was some violence but we were able to change the way American History would be taught to Black students for generations to come. There were so many social issues during the 60s and 70s that deserved attention, and were central to my development as a young lady growing up in America that caused me to want to try to make a difference in the world. Social Work is that kind of helping occupation that attempts to help those in need and can give one a sense of self-satisfaction like no other.

But unfortunately, I came from a family with parents that couldn't really help me to find the answer I needed while growing up. Getting a job and raising a family was what my parents were taught and passed this same kind of "futuristic" thinking along to their children. Though I went to college specifically to major in Sociology, I saw convinced that the only occupation available after graduation would be a social worker.

And, in all fairness, I haven't any problems with becoming a social worker but I really wanted to do more with my life. Being confused and not finding my immediate answers, I dropped out of college and started working a regular job as what else, a secretary. Because no matter what, our high school made sure that its students graduated with a skill. And, to make a long story short, I would up bouncing around until I decided to learn computer programming. This occupation seemed to be the most promising, or at least that's what I thought, and so I decided this to be the way to a very lucrative career.

Chapter 3
Computer programming is not the occupation for me

So after graduation and an eighteen-month evening course, here I was again realizing this was not the occupation for me.

Fortunately for me, this seems to be a good time to enter the field of social work because I've been told that Cleveland State has one of the best programs in the country and I have a lot more determination now. I'm only sorry that it has taken me so long to finally make the decision to follow through with my dream. And I sincerely believe that social work is a good fit for me because as I was growing up, I was genuinely empathic to other people's problems. I am a very good listener and it bothers me that we as a society still have a large portion of the population that does not enjoy all the benefits and privileges that should be a right afforded to every citizen of this country.

There are so many people in our society that can benefit from dedicated social workers, and though I haven't done a lot a volunteering, I have participated and done my share of contributing too many worthwhile organizations. You may say from this that this is not the same as volunteering but I still believe this to be my chosen profession and will not in any way deter me. I understand the problems in the field and, yes, I have worked in a very stressful environment with mean spirited individuals with questionable motives. And I know there is a lot of stress in this field and have heard the horror stories but I am determined this is my chosen field and will not be moved from the path that I have chosen.

When I first began my studies in college, I wanted to major in sociology, but social work will be my major with possibly a minor in sociology. But I'm still learning about the field of social work and I'm not absolutely sure what of my minor will be. I would like very much to do counseling because as I said before, I am a good listener and think I would be a very good counselor possibly in a school setting.

The adolescent years were especially difficult as I recall and I believe school counselors can be extremely helpful at this particular junction in a child's life. Everyone has a path that they must follow and I truly believe this is mine.

Chapter 4
I am a positive force

I believe I can be a positive force in my client's lives and will do my best to give them the best assistance they deserve. Quite often we think we know exactly what someone else needs in their life and yet we may not know exactly what we need in our own. I understand now why often we follow a particular path because we may be missing or lacking something of importance in our own lives. I believe this to be very true or at least in my case it is. I've always wanted to be of assistance to young people because I've felt all along that if I had this kind of help my life may have gone in an entirely different direction when I was growing up.

I believe that adults have the responsibility of teaching, guiding the directing the path of those under their direct supervision. But so often, especially in this enlightened age, adults seem to have lost touch with those that look to them for guidance. As a social worker, I hope to be able to make a difference in someone's life and to possibly be a guiding force for someone that may be considering an occupation in social work.

As a transfer student from Cuyahoga Community College, I am so fortunate to have had some excellent social work professors that were so very encouraging and gave me the incentive to pursue the field of social work. I have to give credit where it is due and would be remiss if I didn't include Dr. Blackmon or as one of my mentors. I was actually pursuing a career in Urban Studies when I found out about the Social Work program at Tri-C and was I excited about being a part of it! I felt as if I had been given a second chance to fulfill my destiny and I'm so glad that I'm a part of this program.

I plan to continue my education through the master's level and hope to receive my bachelor's degree within the next year or so.

This journey has truly been a life changing process for me and has made me that much more determined to complete my goal. The decision to return to college was not so difficult though because I really felt I was up to the challenge. But, changing one's occupation in middle age is a different story altogether. It's very difficult to return to college after so many years but.

Chapter 5

A special child behavior study

The focus of this observation is a seven-year old male named Christian who is of African American descent in late childhood. The age and sex of other siblings are three and six both females. Chris's mother believes that the younger siblings have both a positive and negative influence on him in various ways. For example, because Chris is the older, his younger siblings will often look upon Chris as a leader and sometimes he will take upon the task of giving directions and being the one they look to for answers.

In terms of their negative influence, Chris will sometimes revert back to the baby stage when he sees his younger sibling getting more attention. The socioeconomic status is that of a divorced African American female with three years of college who is working toward a degree in Business. Chris's mom has a position with the Internal Revenue Service that also provides good benefits but unfortunately she receives minimal child support. She receives a great deal of help from her mother and father along with other family members as well as help from social services via food stamps and day care.

The usual care-taking person is the mother who describes Chris as being very loving but very sensitive. Also, she says that Chris can be a handful at time when he's bored and then he can be very aggravating. Chris is in the first grade and spends six and a half hours at school five days a week during a school year, or ten hours a day/five days a week including day camp. Chris spends at least ten hours a day with peers and approximately three hours a day with parents or other adults.

Chris's behavior at school ranges from excellent to good. His mom attributes this change in attitude to the change in the seasons. She believes that during the summer children become more agitated or restless with the advent of summer recess but otherwise Chris is a model student and gets good grades in school. In relation to his attitude and behavior in general, Chris doesn't seem to display any problems in this regard. And as far as extracurricular activities, Chris loves to play football and gets along well with his peers.

In addition, Chris's teachers speak highly of him. In terms of the quality of peer relations, Chris interacts well with other children at the day camp and also has a few close friends that he likes to spend time wish-one at day camp and another who is a neighbor. Although Chris is very easy-going in nature, his male friends tens to bring out the aggressiveness in him when they play together. Chris is very shy in terms of self-esteem but because of his excellent reading ability, his teacher encourages him by giving him special projects.

For example, Chris's teacher gave him the leading role in a television project that aired on the community channel that featured Chris as the male lead. His mother couldn't believe the ease in which Chris performed in this endeavor because of his shyness but attributes it to the fact that Chris likes being the center of attention. His mom stated that she was also very shy but was terrified at his age at having the lead role as the "MC" in her school play. Also, Chris doesn't exhibit any nervous habits but his mom says that when he was much younger he carried a security blanket until the family moved and afterwards never needed it again. Chris has never suffered any physical trauma but did become more attached to his mother when his parent divorced.

According to Chris's mom, Chris has a strong sense of justice or morality and shows deep concern for his younger siblings and relatives as well. Chris doesn't display a conflict with his parent but his mother relates that he has a habit of becoming quite worrisome when he's bored or left idle too long. His mother has to find ways to keep Chris busy so that he doesn't have a lot of idle time. As to the question of physical attractiveness, Chris is a handsome child, very tall for his age with a slim build. Chris likes to select his wardrobe himself, and seems to possess all the characteristics of an intelligent, normal, well-adjusted child and at times display qualities that seem to be well above his years as a child because he seems to be very thoughtful of other people's feelings/needs.

According to Abraham Maslow's hierarchy of needs theory, "people have inborn needs which are arranged in a hierarchy of decreasing importance for survival. According to this theory, and individual must satisfy the most basic needs at the bottom of the hierarchy before the self-actualization process can take place" which is the highest level that a person can achieve. Self-Actualization is described as the ability to be the best that one can be or the best human that one can become. In order to accomplish this, Maslow constructed a list of needs beginning with man's most basic physiological needs such as food, air, water, sleep and sex. Continuing up the ladder, man's need for safety is next in terms of importance, the need for belonging and love, self-esteem needs, and finally arriving at self-actualization. Self-actualization is the highest level that an individual can achieve even though, according to Maslow, very few adults are able to attain this level in their lifetime. Since the basis of this observation study concerns a child's behavior, this paper will not address those needs that are specific to adult behavior but the needs of a child.

For example, according to this theory, the most basic needs for a child would be food, air, water and sleep but not sex. But according to this theory, if a child or adult needs food, there is absolutely nothing more important to him at that moment than being fed. This would also apply to babies who cry instinctively when they are hungry. Once this physiological need is met, the child will go to sleep at peace with the world because his basic needs have been met.

Now that this need has been met, more important needs at a higher level can now be addressed such as man' need for safety. In <u>Motivation and Personality, 1970,</u> Maslow explain that although his theory focuses mainly on adults, one can understand his safety needs approach more efficiently by observing children and infants; and that there are several ways that a child can indicate his need for safety.

For example, Maslow states infants become very distressed if they are disturbed or startled if they hear a loud noise. He explains that children need some kind of undisrupted routine or rhythm. And goes on to say that children seem to want a predictable, lawful, orderly world. In essence, all children need secure stable surroundings that have order, familiarity and is organized and structured. This idea is also emphasized by global in the Third Force, 1970, who states "Child psychologists and teachers have found that children need a predictable world; a child prefers consistency, fairness and a certain amount of routine." This may explain why Chris become more attach to his mother after his parents separated, because he felt insecure in the new situation he found himself in and in essence his world has become unpredictable. Most children look to their parents for protection and due to fear of the unknown. Once a child has worked through safety issues, the need for belonging and love becomes important. Cross and Cross, Knowing Yourself Inside Out, 1998, explains this need as a strong force that can be satisfied through intimate relationships with other people. And states, "The more mobile the society becomes the less the need to belong is satisfied." And further indicates that finding a position in a community, or in a neighborhood, through a group, an organization can provide a sense of belonging.

Most theorists would agree that a child that is shown love on a regular basis and who receives praise would undoubtedly be instilled with the ability to show love and give love as well. A child that is shown love will not grow up with deficiencies that could cripple or impair him in the way he sees the outside world and how he interacts with other people. The fact that Chris is a loving child indicates he has grown up in a loving environment where he is shown respect and kindness. Chris's mom has Chris enrolled in camp (along with his other siblings) during the summer so that Chris would make new friends. Chris has a host of relatives along with friends and fellow classmates; it stands to reason that Chris shouldn't have any reason to feel unloved and does not display negative behavior traits.

Finally, I do not believe that Chris has self-esteem issues because he truly enjoys being the center of attention. This may simply be an indication that his mom needs to reach other areas that Chris may have interest in such as acting, music, skate boarding, etc. In addition, the study seems to indicate Chris and his siblings spends more time away from their mom; and his dad spends very little time with him at all. This could become a self-esteem issue if it weren't for the fact that Chris's mom has made the necessary adjustments in her budget in order to take a government furlough until October. This will allow her to not only spend more time with her children, a specifically Chris, but also complete an on-line course toward a Business degree while they sleep. Of course, lastly on the list of needs is self-actualization which Maslow has indicated can only be accomplished by and adult. This makes perfect sense since my subject (Chris) has yet to deal with identity issues, intimacy and many other issues that will only become manifest as Chris gets older.

For now, Chris needs only to deal with childhood matters such as playing, making friends, and challenging himself whenever possible. And I believe given lots of love, supervision, and guidance, Chris could very easily be on his way to self-actualization.

Chapter 6

How to avoid Burn out as a Social Worker

Attitudes toward Physical Fitness: Which attitude are you?

It is probably a well-known fact by now that Americans have the worst record when it comes to being fit. We simply do not have the same lifestyle as most people in other countries. For most of us, walking is something we don't do unless we have to. The same goes for running. Most of us work in an office and sit all day behind desks.

After work, we retreat into our homes and because our lifestyles are so hectic and the nature of our jobs so stressful, we are usually too tired to venture out again. We have become used to a sedentary lifestyle. Watching television or reading a book is a favorite past time because it helps us to unwind from the day's activities. Because of the difference in cultures and lifestyles, we here in the United States have become lazy and lethargic.

Thankfully, something has been done about this. The President's Council on Fitness was established with just this purpose in mind--to encourage Americans into becoming more fitness conscious. I don't know about you, but I have always been aware of the importance of being fitness conscious and through the years have noticed three prevailing attitudes toward physical fitness.

The first attitude is the saddest because, in this case, this individual is absolutely hopeless. He/she has absolutely no intention of starting an exercise program or anything health related for that matter. This person would drive their car through the grocery store if they could get away with it. The second attitude is the worst case because he/she is a fitness junkie. This individual cannot forego a day without feeling guilty, and will preach and chastise anyone who does not feel the same way. The last attitude is that of someone who knows the importance of a fitness program and finds ways of working it into their daily activities.

I understand the importance of physical fitness and at one time (when I was much younger of course) I would actually do thirty minutes of calestetics before going to work. In the summer months, I would walk to work in the mornings and usually walked home every evening. Being an active person, I played tennis, jogged, and participated in aerobics activities of all kinds including bicycling. Now that I'm older and my schedule a lot more demanding, I must make the time to exercise.

Now the second attitude that I spoke about is the individual who has the right attitude but takes the idea too far. This person is very serious about their fitness program in the worst possible way. This type of attitude suggests an individual who would not think of taking a day out from exercising. You could not keep this person from the gym. He/she will go to the gym everyday for step aerobics classes, etc for at least an hour. And in addition, will spend at least an hour or two in the weight room.

In total, this person will probably spend a couple of hours each day working out. He/she wouldn't dream of going to the gym with anyone who wasn't in perfect physical condition. Every single thought or decision revolves around their exercise program. There is no holiday or family event that is important enough to postpone the daily jaunt to the gym. In other words, this person's whole life revolves around their physical fitness program. It is at this point that this person's attitude toward physical fitness has turned into an obsession, taking precedence over everything and everyone else.

Now the last attitude I'll speak about is the person with the laxidasical attitude who finds every excuse in the world for not starting a fitness program. Oh, they would exercise, or so they say, if they just had someone to exercise with. This individual will visit a gym or spa but will not go back again. They don't need to go to a spa because they have all the exercise equipment at home. But exercise equipment is not the problem. This person has every piece of exercise equipment that has ever been invented. Their exercise room collects dust because they simply have no intention of using it. But they claim that one-day they will get started on an exercise program.

Of course, we know this will never happen. This individual does not see the importance of a fitness program in their life, and have undoubtedly put their own health at risk. With so much attention being given to the subject of physical fitness, there is simply no excuse for being complacent about the matter.

There are numerous paths one can take to becoming physically fit but one must begin somewhere. A physical fitness program can involve the whole family, and there are many ways of including some type of physical exercise in our everyday routine. In addition, a fitness program can be fun. There are numerous videos on the market that offer a fitness program for everyone no matter what physical condition they are in.

Also, the library, bookstore, Internet, newspaper, magazine and television are just a few of the resources that offer a wealth of information on the subject. For me, the hardest part of all was getting started and there were days when I simply had to push myself. Once you get started though, it gets easier and easier. Besides, in the long run the reward will be well worth the effort.

REFERENCES

Cross, J. & Cross, P. B. (1998). <u>Knowing Yourself Inside Out For Self-Direction – Six Theories of Psychology,</u> Crystal Publications: Berkeley.

Maslow, Abraham, H. (1970). <u>Motivation and Personality</u>, Harper & Row, Publishers: New York, Evanston, and London.

Conclusion

I hope you enjoyed this book and it helps you to continue to pursue your dreams.

Thank you and good luck!

Check Out My Other Books

Below you'll find some of my other popular books that are popular on Amazon and Kindle as well. Check them out. Don't forget to leave a review on amazon.com. Thanks

I just want to be "NORMAL"
http://www.amazon.com/just-want-NORMAL-Strategies-Recovery/dp/1505880181

Positive Affirmations for a better life.

http://www.amazon.com/s/ref=nb_sb_n oss?url=search-alias%3Dstripbooks&field-keywords=positive+affrmations+for+a+b etter+life&rh=n%3A283155%2Ck%3Aposi tive+affrmations+for+a+better+life

Coping with Anxiety Disorder. http://www.amazon.com/Coping-Anxiety-Disorder-Tension-illness-ebook/dp/B00X1QXXJ0/ref=sr_1_12?s=b ooks&ie=UTF8&qid=1431051004&sr=1-

**12&keywords=Coping+with+anxiety+diso
rder**

If the links do not work, for whatever reason, you
can simply search for these titles on the Amazon
website to find them.